TWO MOMS IN MY OFFICE DEVOTIONAL

Object lessons from Random Objects

COACH PHIL FARVER

Printed in the United States of America.

Library of Congress Control Number: 2023931598

ISBN   Paperback   979-8-88887-178-2
                 eBook   979-8-88887-179-9

Westwood Books Publishing LLC
Atlanta Financial Center
3343 Peachtree Rd NE Ste 145-725
Atlanta, GA 30326

www.westwoodbookspublishing.com

INTRODUCTION

We began this new school year with a lot of apprehension not knowing what might be in store for us as we were coming out of the Covid-19 pandemic. We did know some things for sure. We knew our enrollment was up, higher than ever before. We knew we had several new staff members both in administration and as teachers. We knew at any time we might shut down because of a flash of the virus. We also knew that God put us in position to be successful and to impact the lives of another group of students. We had a new person in our enrollment department and a new director of marketing. Both are moms with kids in our school. Both have a vested interest in the education and well-being of their children. Both have become very good at the task they have been charged with doing.

We began the year with a meeting on Monday mornings to discuss the events of the previous week and the events of the coming week. We also would take a long range look at whatever big ticket events might be coming up this year. The first meeting was very interesting and I knew that we would get along just fine. Not only could these two moms dish out the flack but they could also take it. We developed a very good relationship and we all looked forward to the Monday meetings. Right off the bat they started in on me about the décor of my office and how it was arranged and continually asked why I had certain things on the shelves or on my desk. It got so they came in and just looked for things to ask about. Somehow the topic of me writing and publishing two books came up, which they said they didn't believe I could do. I told them that I could write a devotional on anything they found in my office and so the challenge was on. They challenged me with an object and before the day was done I had written a devotional and sent it to them. Their challenges were too easy for me as they would rattle off some random object they saw in my office and I would immediately start thinking of how I can make that the object of another devotional. Once I had written four or five of them we took up the challenge to maybe write one for each day of the month and eventually put them in a book and have it published. Thus we have the TWO MOMS IN MY OFFICE DEVOTIONAL.

Responsibilities have changed and one of them moved into a different role and doesn't come to the meetings on Mondays anymore. The other still meets with me on Mondays, we still talk about the previous week events and games. We still look at the calendar for upcoming events and games. She still challenges me, picking out random objects to see if I can step up to the task. We have developed a great friendship and I love both of them like a sister. My hope and prayer is that something you read in these pages will be an inspiration to you, maybe even motivate you to take a step in a different direction and become more for Him than you were before.

Coach Phil Farver

FOREWORD

If someone were to ask me, tell me about somebody you know that you feel really *loves* coaching – my answer would be – my friend Phil Farver. It's hard to believe that Phil and I first met thirty years ago here at Indian Rocks Christian School. The amazing thing to me is that he has steered the athletic department at IRCS the entire time! It is an example of his commitment and loyalty to his school and his craft.

His lengthy tenure is unusual in today's environment. It is in itself, a remarkable achievement! Phil has numerous accomplishments during these thirty years, but if you were to ask him, he would say it is not about the recognition. It's about the players and the enduring relationships that have resulted. As you read the pages of this book you will undoubtedly get a glimpse into the "heart" of Coach Farver. I am blessed to have worked alongside of him and I hope this book will inspire and motivate you as you lead others.

Rob Starner

True greatness comes when we recognize to do right; in spite of the consequences and regardless of the circumstances, because it is the right thing to do.

ACKNOWLEDGEMENTS

I want to thank my family for loving me and putting up with an old coach who loves deeply and strives to be a winner in everything. My wife, Rhonda, is the greatest blessing in my life. She has been the best assistant coach a guy could ask for. My children Kindal and Blake, the next best blessings in my life, along with their spouses, Danny and Alexa. I also want to acknowledge the three littles that help Pop pop keep going, Asher James, Ivy Joy and Layla Lou. This book wouldn't have even been a thought without the two moms who helped inspire me to write it and were great influences on the content, thank you Jillian and Mayli. Thank you for challenging me in your own special ways. I hope you continue to be a blessing in the roles you fill wherever you may be. Most importantly, thank you Lord, for allowing me the opportunity to write and to share some simple truths from the random objects found in everyday life.

If we don't take control of our life,
don't complain when others do.

Beth Mende Conny

BIBLE

This is my study Bible and it is the New Living Translation. I use it for all my studying when I prepare a message for chapel, a devotion for faculty meetings or my basketball team and when I write devotionals for my books. I find that it is very easy to read and brings home a point very clearly as God intended. I have many favorite passages and verses as I have tried to apply the principles of His Word to my life. I found a very interesting passage in Isaiah 43:1-4

> *"But now, O Israel, the Lord who created you says: Do not be afraid, for I have ransomed you. I have called you by name; you are mine. When you go through deep waters and great trouble, I will be with you. When you go through rivers of difficulty, you will not drown! When you walk through the fire of oppression, you will not be burned up; the flames will not consume you. For I am the Lord, your God, the Holy One of Israel, your Savior. I gave Egypt, Ethiopia, and Seba as a ransom for your freedom. Others died that you might live. I traded their lives for yours because you are precious to me. You are honored and I love you."*

I find so many things to unpack in these verses, yet I only want to touch them on the surface. Maybe I can go deeper in another devotional. I find here that I am honored and loved by the One who created me. I find His watchcare and provision for me.

1. God takes us thru deep waters – because the enemy can't swim; to teach us not to look around at the circumstances and to teach us to trust Him.

2. God puts us into rivers of difficulty – he promises us we will not drown and to teach us to stand strong against the flow of the world.

3. God takes us through the fires of oppression – to purify us like gold, to harden us like steel, building strong character within us.

The end game is to know God better and become more like His Son in all aspects of our lives.

BOOKS

I always liked to read. When I was a kid I would go to bed at night with a flashlight under the blankets and read a book. Mostly those books were sports books, either biographies of great players or just stories about sports. Baseball was always a favorite of mine. I read about Jackie Robinson, Mickey Mantle, Babe Ruth, Lou Gehrig, Ty Cobb and others. My favorite book of all time was called, "The Southpaw Flyhawk". I must have read that book twenty times over. I read these stories and got so engrossed in them that I virtually put my self in the setting. I would dream about being the main character in the book I was reading. As I have grown older my reading taste has become more diversified. Certainly I still enjoy the sports biographies, but I really enjoy biographies in general. I like books about historical events, self-help books, books about coaching, and books with curious titles. I love to read books written by John Maxwell, Mark Miller and Jim Collins. I especially like all of John Wooden's books.

Books are important they give instruction, they give insight and they give out information. Books tell a story. I heard it said, "Every number has a name, every name has a story and every story matters to God". I enjoy reading about and listening to the stories of people and the struggles they have overcome and even those they didn't overcome. Some are triumphant and some are tragic, but all have purpose and meaning.

When you think you are nothing, that your life doesn't have a purpose, no one cares about who you are or what you do.....STOP!! Nothing could be farther from the truth. You are a living being created in the image of God. Your life matters to God. He created you, He gave you talents and abilities, He put within you a specific purpose. Maybe you just haven't found it yet, but it is there. You MATTER to God. The best thing you can do is to pick up THE BOOK and immerse yourself in it, seeking God in a way that you never have before. God's Word, the Bible, tells stories, gives instruction, tells us how to live, tells us what to avoid, gives us advice and more importantly tells us how much God loves us and cares for us.

> II Timothy 3:16-17 – *All scripture is inspired by God and is useful to teach us what is true and to make us realize what is wrong in our lives. It straightens us out and teaches us to do what is right. It is God's way of preparing us in every way, fully equipped for every good thing God wants us to do."*

If you find yourself struggling with everyday life and finding purpose for your own existence, pick up your BIBLE and search for what God wants for you and from you.

The two moms visited my office again this week to discuss the activities of the week so we can be better prepared. As they diligently scoured my office trying to find the next object for our devotions, their eyes landed on an odd object. I have a bowling pin on my bookshelf and that is what they challenged me to use in this week's devotional.

The bowling pin has some history to it and has a significant place in Indian Rocks Athletic lore. That is one of the actual bowling pins used in the FHSAA State competition in 2005. That year our bowling team became the first to qualify for the State tournament in Orlando. If memory serves me correctly, we had a couple outstanding bowlers on the team that year. In fact one of them recorded the only perfect game in the history of the school. 300! The closest I have ever been to a 300 game I believe was a 281. Wow! 300! That is amazing.

When I look at the bowling pin I see on it scuffs, scraps and scars from being knocked down over and over again. I suppose the life span of a bowling pin depends upon the pin staying intact without any cracks or breaks. As many times as that bowling pin gets knocked down, something or someone is there to stand it back up again. It makes me think of our lives in general. We are faced with trials and tribulations over and over again, even to the point where we are knocked down. But true to His character, Jesus is always there with an outstretched hand to pick us up, dust us off, and pat us on the back. He tells us everything is okay and to keep going.

> II Corinthians 4:8-9 tells us exactly that, *"We are pressed on every side by troubles, but we are not crushed and broken. We are perplexed, but we don't give up and quit. We are hunted down, but God never abandons us. We get knocked down, but we get up again and keep going"*

Don't look at the circumstances around you, don't fret over the waves coming at you, don't worry about tomorrow, and don't look for an easy way out. If you get knocked down, with God's help, get up and keep going.

BOXING GLOVE

I do not remember who gave me this boxing glove or when it was given to me. It did come with credentials though, stating that the signatures were authentic. It was signed by two of the great Ernies to have graced the boxing world: Ernie Holmes and Ernie Shavers. Both of these guys were in the heavyweight division of boxing during the time when boxing was in its prime. They shared the spotlight with many famous boxers of that era: Joe Frazier, Mohammed Ali, Thomas Hearns, Sugar Ray Leonard, and others. The art and the sport of boxing have basically given way to MMA, a combination of boxing, wrestling, jujitsu, karate, judo and everything else creating a blood sport that is popular around the world. There is something all these famous fighters had in common; They fought with a purpose. They trained hard and had laser-like focus in achieving their goals: to be the best in the world in their division. Growing up I watched many fights matching some of the world's top boxers in the ring. I saw some who were strong and could just outpunch everyone. I saw some who were deliberate and had a game plan to follow. I saw some who fought with finesse and class, I also saw some who were despised for their attitudes and their approach to boxing. In fact there have been some who were disqualified from a match due to their actions.

I Corinthians 9:25-27 *"All athletes practice strict self-control. They do it to win a prize that will fade away, but we do it for an eternal prize. So I run straight to the goal with purpose in every*

*step. I am not like a boxer who misses his punches. I discipline my
body like an athlete training it to do what it should."*

We do not live wildly but with purpose. We do not fight against unknown
opponents, but rather we fight against the flesh and the devil. We don't
live our lives like hell during the week and then act like a righteous Joe on
Sunday. Paul reminds us that we should live in such a way that when we
preach or teach others about following Christ that we are not disqualified
due to our attitudes and actions. But rather our lives serve as a living
sacrifice, being an example of humility and servanthood to God and
man. We live disciplined lives so that others may see God in us.

CALENDAR

I know you won't believe me but I can tell the future.

Taking another clue from random objects in my office, I have had this 36 year calendar on my desk for as long as I can remember. I don't even remember where I got it or who gave it to me. It is a pretty neat little calendar though. I can tell you what day any date from now through 2036 will fall on.

I know that in our finite minds, many people are curious as to the future and what is going to happen. I have read stories of people wanting to know the day they will die and how they will die. Some want to know to do whatever they can do to avoid that date. Others want to know because they would change the way they are living so they can finish this life on a strong note. I don't know if I really want to know that information. It seems kind of morbid to me.

Being a believer in and follower of Jesus Christ, I really don't have to worry about any of that. I know what my future holds and who holds my future. We sometimes get so caught up in the here and now and worry about the storms and waves around us that we tend to forget the very fact that God has us in the palm of His hand.

The only impact we can possibly have on the future is to live each day to the fullest in serving God and serving others. These are the two things

I am responsible for in life. I pray that I do them well every day. I know that I have failed many times over and will fail many times to come. But if I strive to do them well, to the best of my God given abilities and talents then I will be successful in life. I hope one day to hear, "Well done".

> Jeremiah 29:11, *"For I know the plans I have for you, says the Lord. They are plans for good and not for disaster, to give you a future and a hope."*

In Christ alone I find a future and a hope.

CANDLE

I love candles! Especially those that are scented. I have burned some candles that have a very nice scent, like my favorite vanilla or French vanilla. That is my absolute all time favorite. I have also burned some candles that I could not wait to extinguish and throw away because the scent was awful! Why in the world would anyone think that certain scents are good in a candle?

There are three things that I have observed about burning candles:

1. They give off fragrance. Well, only if they are scented candles, but for the purpose of our devotional we are talking about scented candles. Some are very aromatic, sweet and pleasant. Some are strong and overbearing. Some others can be repugnant. Our lives should be like a sweet fragrance to God as we live each day to serve and to love Him and those around us.

2. They give warmth. Now, it would take several very large candles to warm up a house and that in itself may be a fire hazard. There was a day in time that houses were heated by fireplace or wood burning stoves. We are spoiled, flick a switch and we have heat. Being a friend is like being a candle, you should have a warm personality, ready to help your friends in their hour of need.

3. They give off light. I cannot imagine the day in time when all they had was light by candles, fireplaces and oil lamps. Wow are we totally spoiled, just flick a switch and we have light. The Bible tells us that we are like a candle or a lamp and we should shine our light so others can see God's handiwork in us.

- Matthew 5:14-16 *"You are the light of the world – like a city on a mountain, glowing in the night for all to see. Don't hide your light under a basket! Instead, put it on a stand and let it shine for all, In the same way, let your good deed shine out for all to see, so that everyone will praise your heavenly Father."*

We don't shine so others will see us and tell us how great we are, we shine so that others will see God and praise Him.

CHAMPION

CHAMPION. What is a champion? According to Webster's dictionary a champion is defined as follows:

1. a winner of first prize or first place in competition
2. one who shows marked superiority
3. a militant <u>advocate</u> or defender
4. WARRIOR, FIGHTER
5. one that does battle for another's rights or honor

When I read these definitions I can't help but to think about the movie TROY. Toward the beginning of the movie two great armies come face to face for battle. In those days, rather than risk the loss of many lives, each king would select a "champion" from among his troops to fight one on one. The army whose "champion" would defeat the other would win the battle and the losing army would become subservient to the winning army. Agamemnon summoned his champion, Achilles to fight against a bigger stronger looking opponent. In one move, his patented move, Achilles killed his opponent and thus won the battle for the Greeks. They later would go against Troy in the long lasting Trojan war. And you know the rest of the story.

Biblically two persons come to mind when I think of a champion. You may have others come to your mind and that's okay. I choose these two men as champions. First there was Samson. His life was on a roller coaster ride and hit the low point when he couldn't resist Delilah. But in his death he conquered his enemies through his God given strength. David is the other champion that comes to minds. Starting with the killing of Goliath, David was a man after God's own heart and was the champion God chose to lead the nation of Israel.

In sports and in life, we are given an opportunity every day to be a champion. We should approach each day with purpose and focus to be the best we can be that day. Whether it be on the field, the court, in the office, at school or home. Champions never quit, they never waver and they face their enemies straight on. Be a champion today.

COW BELL

Funny that you would find a Cow Bell on my shelf and then challenge me to write about it. One of our player's mom made these cow bells to celebrate winning the District Championship in 2005. She made sure to give me one and I have kept it on my shelf all this time. It is a great reminder of that team and the successes of that season. Our fans were very supportive that year and made a lot of noise in cheering for the girls. Now, they could not use the cow bells because it is against the rules to have artificial noise makers in the gym during the games. However, they did come in handy for after the game and for pep rallies. You always hear "you need more cow bells" at professional games. You can hear the sound without even hearing the sound, if you know what I mean. You know what the cow bell sounds like. It is loud and can be obnoxious, just a lot of noise, no substantial contribution to the game itself. Just noise.

Paul tells us in I Corinthians 13, the "Love Chapter", that if he had all the signs and gifts in the world but didn't have love he would be nothing but noise. A loud gong or clanging cymbal. Meaning you can talk all you want but if your walk doesn't match your talk. It is just noise. Loving God and loving others is general theme to this portion of scripture. Paul says that if he, if we didn't love others then he, we would be of no value. I have said before that we may be the only Jesus someone we cross paths with may ever see. Paul tells us in Romans 12:9, "*Don't just pretend that you love others, REALLY love them*".

Later in the chapter he says, *"Love each other with genuine affection, and take delight in honoring each other"*.

Don't be THAT person who can talk the talk but what you say just falls on deaf ears because you are just noise. We need more "cow bell" Christians who ring out the good news loud and clear, then live it to the best of their ability.

EAGLE

There are some objects in my office that present a challenge just to write a devotional about. There are some that are obvious and very easy to develop. Then there are objects that present several different paths I could take in developing a devotional. This eagle is one of those objects.

This is my 30th year as the Athletic Director here at Indian Rocks Christian School and our mascot has been the Golden Eagle. We are transitioning to just "Eagles" as it makes it much easier for cheers, uniforms, school apparel, etc. This eagle was a Christmas present from one of my basketball girls from several years ago. It has a very special significance for me in remembering past players and teams as well as remembering who we are in Christ. The inscription on the base says, "They shall mount up with wings as Eagles", which in itself creates a very easy path for a devotional. The reference is from II Chronicles 7:14.

> *"Then if my people who are called by my name will humble themselves and pray and seek my face and turn from their wicked ways, I will hear from heaven and will forgive their sins and heal their lands"*

There is a 4 for 3 offer here. At that time God's people as referenced here were the Israelites. The nation was all over the place in their relationship with God. When they really worshipped Him and followed Him they were blessed beyond measure. The biggest problem was that they would stray from the truth and get complacent in their relationship with Him. Much like us today. We get our eyes off from what really matters and are distracted by the world around us. When that happens our hearts take on a cold nature and we slip away from God and the path he intends for us.

There are four things God asks of us when we find ourselves straying: first to humble ourselves (realize that we are off path and have a need to get on the right path), second is that we need to pray. Prayer is a very powerful thing and can change the world. Third is to seek God and fourth is to turn, do a 180 and head in the right direction. When we do that, God says he will hear us, forgive us and heal us. It is pretty simple, and yet man has made the path to God seem impossible.

Don't be a turkey and run with the crowd, be an eagle and fly above the world today!

DEVOTIONAL

This little guy is the object that the two moms challenged me with for a devotional this week. It's funny because there are so many thoughts that come to mind when I am looking at it, that it is difficult to narrow in on one path. However, the one thing that does come to mind is this:

> We are not what we do, we are who we are in Christ and
> He is the one from whom we should gain our acceptance.

According to Psalm 139 - God made us, he designed us, He knows us from top to bottom. He knows what He designed us to do and He knows what we are capable of doing, both good and bad. He knows we will make mistakes and He knows that we will fail time and again. And yet, because we are His child, He stands with open arms waiting to take us in to Himself every single day, every single time that we do stumble and fail.

Too many times we work very hard to find our identity in what we do here on earth instead of focusing on who we are because of Him. A simple little toy football with outstretched arms reminds me daily that even though I fail, even though I sin and even though I may lose a game as a coach, the world is not going to end. If we turn to our Creator and rest in Him, we find where our true identity lies. God is the only one who is qualified to define our identity. Don't allow others opinions to shape your identity, but see yourself as God sees you.

Our devotional challenge this week is once again a result of the curiosity of Two Moms looking around my office and asking what is that? Asking why do you have that in here? Where did you get that? This week they noticed a spray bottle of Sandalwood/Patchoulis scent, used to bring a nice manly fragrance to the ambiance of my office.

> In John 12:3, *"Then Mary took a twelve ounce jar of expensive perfume made from essence of nard and she anointed Jesus' feet with it and wiped his feet with her hair. And the house was filled with fragrance."*

Mary had a very expensive box/jar/vessel made from alabaster which is a marble like stone. In that vessel she had a very, very expensive oil known as nard or spikenard. This oil was from Northern India, it was a sacred Himalayan essence used for medicinal purposes for the nervous system, sleeping problems, cardiac rhythm problem, psoriasis and for burials. The oil that Mary used was worth something like 300 denarii or about $55,000 in US money. She had it, no doubt, to use for her own burial. For her to use this oil on Jesus was a great sacrifice on her part to show her love and devotion to her friend and later to be known as her Savior. The oil had a unique fragrance to it and the Bible says that the house was filled with that fragrance, much like using this spray fills the office with a nice smelling fragrance.

II Corinthians 2:14-16 says, *"......Now wherever we go He uses us to tell others about the Lord and to spread the Good News like a sweet perfume. Our lives are a fragrance presented by Christ to God. But this fragrance is perceived differently by those being saved and by those perishing. To those who are perishing we are a fearful smell of death and doom. But to those who are being saved we are a life-giving perfume."*

When in the presence of others, do we give off a scent of negativism, griping and complaining or do our lives have a life-giving fragrance of Christ that will draw others to Him.

HEROES

This was a centerpiece from a patriotic program that we had at our school. I really loved the program and I wanted to keep something as a reminder to me of the freedoms we have because of the heroes who have given their lives for that freedom. There are so many men and women whose stories have or have not been told, that the whole could not be contained in a hundred volumes of writing. Heroes come in all shapes, sizes, age and abilities. You never had to look very far to find one. It is all in your perspective of what a hero is and who represents that perspective in your own mind. I'll bet we could sit and talk about this for days and days, recounting heroic actions and events that have impacted our lives. I have often said that my dad was my hero. Even now that he has gone on to be with the Lord, I consider him to be my hero.

My dad was the closest example of God that I have ever known. He was strong yet tender. He had large hands and I would often think that his hands were what God's hands looked like. You didn't mess with my dad because I thought he could whoop up on everybody, but he was a gentle and loving caregiver. He was a giver almost to a fault, we didn't have much growing up in a small Midwestern church setting but our home was always open for one more mouth to feed or one more person in need. He loved to preach, loved his family and loved the Detroit Tigers. I can remember watching games with him and he would be yelling at the team on the television. Just the thought of that makes me chuckle even now. My dad was not perfect but he was the perfect dad for me and my siblings. He instilled in us a work ethic, a love, a caring attitude and a sense of pride in who we are and what we represent. I love my dad and miss him very much.

The Bible is full of heroes both large and small. Hebrews 11 talks about some of the heroes of faith. Life is full of heroes both large and small. Let us always remember those who have gone before us and blazed the trail for us to walk upon freely.

WHO IS YOUR HERO AND WHY?

CAN OF COKE

Most of the things that the Two Moms find in my office are obscure things, little things on my book shelf or hanging on the wall. This time they really thought there is no way he can do a devotional on a commemorative can of Coca Cola.

Well, as I thought about developing a devotional on this item there were two things that came to mind. First the can of coke itself. I think back to a slogan that Coca Cola had years ago stating: "It's the real thing."

Coca Cola has been around for many years. The company was founded in the 1880's by Asa Griggs Candler. He bought the original recipe for the drink from chemist John Smith Pemberton in Atlanta, Georgia, for a reported sum of $238.98. The drink was made up of coca leaf extract, caffeine, carbonated water and sugar. It was advertised as a relief for mental and physical fatigue and a cure for headaches. In 1903 Candler removed the cocaine portion and sold that to pharmaceutical companies. In 1919 he sold the company for a reported $25,000,000. Quite the return on his initial investment I would say.

There have been many slogans over the years and in 1969 the slogan was, "IT'S THE REAL THING". People today are searching for answers, they are searching for peace in their lives, they are searching for love and they are searching for something they can hang on to that will give them hope. The world offers temporal things as stated in I John 2:16, "For the world offers only the lust for physical pleasure, the lust for everything we see and pride in our possessions. These are not from the Father. They are from this evil world". What the world offers is not "the real thing". It is only temporary. It is like a vapor that appears for a little while then disappears.

> John 3:16, *"For God, so loved the world that he gave his only begotten son. That whosoever believeth on him would not perish but have eternal life." God offers us eternity with him. God offers us abundant life. God offers us what amounts to THE REAL THING.*

What are you searching for today? Put your faith and trust in Jesus Christ and receive THE REAL THING.

ON THE LEVEL

You know, as I was sitting here in my office talking to a couple moms this morning, one of them asked me why I have a level on my bookcase. Being of quick wit, I answered it is there so when I look at it I am reminded to be level headed and even keeled on a daily basis.

> **I Peter 3:8-9 says**, *"Finally, all of you should be of one mind, full of sympathy toward each other, loving one another with tender hearts and humble minds. Don't repay evil for evil. Don't retaliate when people say unkind things about you. Instead, pay them back with a blessing. This is what God wants you to do, and he will bless you for it."*

There are definitely days that I need to look at that level to be reminded of what it represent…maybe 5-6 times a day. I don't want my life to be tipped one way or another, I want to keep that bubble in the middle so that I can be a testimony and an encouragement to everyone on both sides, not just cater to one side or another. I can only do that when I fill my mind with Scripture and put that Scripture to work. It is INTENTIONAL LIVING. It is something I strive for but have failed many times. The great thing about the Lord is that he is always there to balance things out for me when that bubble tips to one side or the other. Realizing it is because of HIS goodness that we are able to stay on the "level".

LIGHT

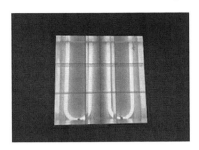

So, when you walk into my office the light is either on or off, pretty simple. When the light is on, there is activity in the office. I am working or counselling or just piddling around reading and writing. When the light is off, there is nothing going on, it is darkened because of the absence of light.

> Jesus said, *"I am the light of the world. If you follow me you won't be stumbling through the darkness, because you will have the light that leads to life."* John 8:12

This is a dark and demented world in which we live and the need for light is greater today than in any other time in history. God says we are a light in this dark world and we need to keep shining so that others will see God working through us. We may be the only light, the only "Jesus" someone will ever see.

1. Saturate your life with TRUTH – John 8:32
    - Think on Good things
    - Read your Bible daily
    - Read good books
    - Watch what goes into your heart thru your eyes and ears

2. Stand firm in your FAITH – Ephesians 6:10-18
    - Don't compromise
    - Set your standards
    - Don't give in
    - Refuse to lose

3. Serve God with your LIFE – Luke 10:27
    - Love God
    - Love Others

LISTEN UP

Of course I have a whistle in my office, I am a coach! Whistles are used by coaches to get someone's attention, to stop action and to begin action. Funny thing about the whistle, I rarely use one in practice. When my teams see me walk into practice with a whistle, they know it is going to be THAT kind of practice. When we want to get the attention in the cafeteria through all the noise, chatter and clatter we blow a whistle. When the work day is completed in a factory a whistle blows signifying the end of the shift. When we line our team up for a drill we blow the whistle to begin. When a referee spots a foul or a violation they blow the whistle to stop the action. When the whistle blows, everyone stops and listens.

God doesn't necessarily use a whistle to get our attention but he does have attention getters that might be called a "whistle". It is very important that we develop the skill of listening. Men probably more than anyone. I have found that when I listen and put into practice what I listen to, then life is much more pleasant. (This is where I have to admit that if I would listen to my wife a little more then I would avoid getting into trouble.) This is also true of God and His Word: if we would read, listen and apply then we would avoid many mistakes and enjoy the kind of life God intended for us to have.

Deuteronomy 27:9   *"… be quiet and listen!"*

I Samuel 15:22   *"Listen! Obedience is better than sacrifice and submission is better than offering the fat of rams"*

Job 15:17   *"If you will listen, I will show you."*

Proverbs 1:33   *"But all those who listen to me will live in peace."*

Mark 4:24   *"Pay close attention to what you hear. The closer you listen, the more understanding you will be given."*

James 1:22   *"Don't just listen to God's Word. You must do what it says."*

Hearing is the ability to perceive sounds by detecting vibrations, listening is putting into practice what you perceive through hearing. I can hear sounds but if I don't LISTEN to them they are nothing more than noise.

LOVE, LOVE, LOVE

The Two Moms are ever so curious as to the different things that I have in my office. Each and every thing has some significance to it. This cute little Valentine's teddy bear was a little something given to me by my daughter when she was very young.

We tried to have children for the first 10 ½ years of our marriage. We suffered through a miscarriage and a failed adoption. We went to every doctor there was trying to find the problem and a remedy so we could have children. One day my dad called and told us a young lady in his church was going to have a baby and knew she couldn't keep it, so she wanted to know if he knew someone that would be a candidate for parenting this little one when she came into the world. We were ecstatic when we got that news and of course said yes. Kindal Noel was born on December 26, 1989, and she was in our arms and our home on December 28. Needless to say she grew up a "daddy's girl", almost to a fault. She grew up at our school, played volleyball and played basketball for her dad. We have had the usual conflicts in the growing years, but we survived and we continue to have a great relationship. She can call on me for help and I will always be there to do what I can do to help her. Now she has a little girl, Layla, who has taken her place and is Pop Pops' girl! Ah the circle of life, gotta love it.

This token of a little girl's love her daddy constantly reminds me of the never ending, unchanging love God has for all of us. He is always there to comfort us to guide us and to lift us up. I John clearly tells us that, "GOD IS LOVE" In fact, He loved us so much that he gave His only son to die for us in order to give us eternal life. My dad always had a sign on the front of his pulpit that said

GIVING DEMONSTRATES YOUR LOVE

I cannot think of a greater sacrifice and a greater gift than what our Heavenly Father gave to each of us. In return we should also demonstrate our love for others.

> Romans 12:9-10 says, *"Don't just pretend that you love others. Really love them. Hate what is wrong, stand on the side of the good. 10 Love each other with genuine affection and take delight in honoring each other."*

MEASURING UP

Growing up today is so much more difficult than it was 50 years ago when I was growing up. Life seemed to be so simple then. We had a rotary dial phone attached to the wall, we were able to get 5-6 channels on the television once we turned the antenna to face the right way, and we ate meals together as a family. We had books to read, encyclopedias for information and research, bicycles to get around on and deliver papers on our route. We went outside to play at 8:00 in the morning and came home for dinner at 5:00. We drank from the hose when we were thirsty and we played baseball in different yards in the neighborhood representing a circuit of "stadiums" that we played. It didn't take much to measure up to the simple standards of the day.

Today is so much different and many times I feel sorry for our kids because they have social media, instant access to information and news, instant meals and they are on the go, go, go all the time. It seems like they never take the time to enjoy simpler things like taking a walk on the beach, watching a sunset, observing nature, enjoying a good book or simply just enjoying the company of friends while playing table games.

Now our kids have to deal with body shaming and gender identity. They are always comparing themselves to the fads and fashions of the world around them. They are judged by how they "measure up" to the standards that society has set for them. Romans 12:1 tells us not to be conformed to this world but be transformed by the renewing of our minds, or change the way we think. Change the standards by which we measure ourselves. In the final analysis of life, the only thing that matters is how we measure up to the standards that God has set for us. The way I see it and read it, there are two major categories of standards set for us. If we do these well we will have accomplished a lot in our lifetime. Those two standards are:

LOVE GOD
LOVE OTHERS.

Everything else in life falls into these two standards. How do you measure up to the standards God has for us? It is never too late to change your thinking and transform yourself to meet His standards.

MILESTONES

Milestones are events that take place in our lives that are significant and have special meaning either to you personally or for your family, team or work place. I have been coaching for 44 years now and there have been some significant milestones in my coaching career. I have had some great teams in the past. One of the milestones that comes to mind was a State Championship we won in the Alabama Private School Association. That team was one of the best teams I have ever coached. I have reminders of win milestones in my career of 100, 200 and so on. One special one for me was depicted here in this picture was that of 600th win. This is significant to me because both my kids and both the grandbabies were present for this game. Now the grandbabies won't remember anything but the stories told about the game, but they were there. These wins and these milestones in coaching are great but they can never be achieved without the help of others. I have never turned the ball over, never taken a shot, never played defense in a game and never shot game winning free throws. Well at least not physically. I have done all this and more in my mind and emotionally. Any coach can attest to that. It took a "TEAM" to accomplish these milestones and I am forever grateful to all the players, both girls and boys who played for me and contributed to the accomplishments.

We all have spiritual milestones in our lives as well. Some of my God ordained milestones:

1. Gave my life to the Lord when I was 7 years old, in 1963.
2. Got baptized by my dad when soon after in Sparlingville, Michigan.
3. Led VBS at our church in Elba, Michigan as a 17 year old.
4. Recommitted my life to the Lord when I went to College at Maranatha Baptist Bible College.
5. Committed to Christian service as a teacher and coach in 1978
6. Married my Christian wife in 1979
7. Adopted our first baby, Kindal, in 1990.
8. Had our second baby, Blake in, 1991.
9. Finishing up my 30th year at Indian Rocks Christian School as coach and Athletic Director.

Philippians 3:13-14 *"No dear brothers and sisters, I am still not all I should b, but I am focusing all my energies on this one thing: Forgetting the past and looking forward to what lies ahead, I strain to reach the end of the race and receive the prize for which God, through Christ Jesus is calling us up to heaven."*

NEMATODES AND MOLE CRICKETS

This is a picture of left field of our baseball field. We have had an infestation of nematodes and mole crickets. Nematodes are worm like creatures that you can't really see except for the damage they do. They eat up the roots of grasses and plants, thus stunting any growth. Mole Crickets are just that, cricket like critters that also dine on roots and on the grass blades. A lot of times the damage these pests cause is not evident until we get something that looks like this. While they are eating the roots beneath the surface, the damage to the surface is intensified as you put more and more stress on it through constant activities. That is why it is important to have good, quality pest control to maintain an athletic field good irrigation and use management come in handy as well.

This brings to mind our daily spiritual lives. When we allow the sin to fester in our lives and go unconfessed, the root of our relationship suffers. The more activities we are involved in and the more we load on ourselves externally eventually manifests itself in a corroded barren life. I think it is safe to say that the Apostle Paul gives many examples in Scripture of the "nematodes" and "mole crickets" that can creep into our lives. In Galatians 5:19-21 we find one of the lists of things that can crawl into our lives and cause major destruction. Things like sexual immorality, impure thought, lustful desires, idolatry, demonic activities, hostility, quarreling, jealousy, anger, selfish ambition, divisiveness, envy, drunkenness and all kinds of other sin.

We can control these spiritual nematodes and mole crickets by reading God's Word, spending quality time with other believers, and controlling our involvement in too many activities that pull us away and distract us from taking care of ourselves.

OPEN DOOR

I have this picture hanging in my office and it depicts the door to the coach's office being open for players to enter in at any time. This picture is one that I have tried to live by for my entire career in coaching. My door is always open and I will drop what I am doing to address a problem, situation or just to chit chat with my players. I have had kids come to my office who never played for me just to talk, to get advice, or to share a burden they are struggling with. I have had players pray and accept Jesus as their Savior in my office. I have had players confess to some pretty deep sin in my office. I have had players come to me and tell me they were pregnant before they have even told their parents. I had a player whose father hung himself in their garage and I was there to wake him up to tell him the tragic event. My door has always been open and I credit that to two big influences in my life. The first influence is my dad. I watched him love on people and provide for their needs even in times that we as a family were needy. We were always willing to share what we had. I am very much like my dad in that respect. He is gone now and I can only hope I am half the man that he was and that all his good qualities live on in me. The other influence is John Wooden. I had the privilege of hearing him speak at a basketball clinic back in 1981 here in Tampa. I have read all his books and admire him so much. The thing that sticks out about him for me is that he had an open Bible on his desk and many players have asked about it and asked about his faith as they sat across from him in his office. His door was always open and his life was always open as an example of how to conduct yourself as a player and as a man.

You know God our Creator and Heavenly Father also has an open door policy. Because of His Son Jesus and His sacrifice, we are able to communicate directly with Him. We don't have to do sacrifices, we don't have to go thru a pastor or a priest, we can go directly to Him. He wants us to develop that relationship with Him. Evan though HE already knows our struggles and our weaknesses, He wants us to tell Him and to seek Him with all of our heart. Take advantage of hooking into the power of God through His Son Jesus. Use this opportunity to have an open door and open life so that you might impact the lives of those who cross your path. There are no accidental meetings, they are all ordained by God for a specific purpose. Be that door that ushers someone into His presence.

PLANT

I have this plant in my office. It is green and stays beautifully green all year long. It has never had any dry leaves, it has never required any fertilizer, special care or even water for that matter. This plant is a fake, it's plastic. I really should get rid of it and have a real live plant. One that requires care. One that experiences growth and everything that goes with growing.

> Luke 2:52 says, *"Jesus grew in wisdom and in stature, and in favor with God and all the people". Jesus wasn't fake, he was real. He set the example for us in every aspect of life. Here we find that He grew in four different ways, different areas that helped complete Him as a human being, as the Son of God.*

We too are His children and we too should be growing in the same four areas of our lives.

First we find that He grew in wisdom. He grew intellectually. We need to do the same, grow intellectually. We do this by reading. Reading His word. Reading good books. Reading good articles. Taking in knowledge then applying that knowledge on a daily basis. That is what wisdom is: knowing what to do with what you know.

Second we find he grew in stature. He grew physically. Now in this passage it is referring to Jesus as a boy growing up, so naturally He grew physically from a boy to a man. We all have grown from being children to being adults, or are in the process of doing so. Some of us have grown a little too much, if you know what I mean. I have been working on growing stronger, growing more healthy and growing smaller.

Third we see that He grew in favor with God. He grew spiritually. He had a natural relationship with his Father but He also nurtured and intentionally lived for that relationship. We need to grow spiritually and we do this by spending time in our relationship with God. Reading His word, hanging out with His people, seeking to serve others as Jesus did.

Fourth we see Jesus grew in favor with the people. He grew relationally. Although the people at the time were seeking for a "king", for someone to deliver them from their physical bondage, Jesus lived where the people were. He spent time healing, providing, caring and building relationships. He was a servant leader.

What a great role model Jesus was for us. Seek to grow in all four areas of your life and you will be a complete person, one whom God has great plans to make prosperous and successful.

5 STONES

About 12 years ago I wrote and published a book, "Five Smooth Stones". The basic premise of the book was based off the David and Goliath story and put into the context of building a team using 5 simple concepts. These "stones" when used properly, will be an asset to anyone's personal life or in the corporate setting of any business or sports teams. The concepts are:

1. Bring your "A" game everyday
2. Treat others the way you want to be treated
3. Leave things better than when you found them
4. Little things make a difference
5. Inspire others to greatness

The stones pictured were given to me by a fellow faculty member after they had read the book. They came upon these stones in a bookstore somewhere and thought they would be a nice gift and reminder of the book. I have kept them on my desk ever since. They each have a Scripture verse etched in them. The Scripture verses serve as reminders of how we can defeat Satan and the world in our daily living.

Psalm 46:10	*"Be still and know that I am God."*
Psalm 62:1	*"My soul finds rest in God, alone."*
Matthew 19:46	*"God can do all things."*
2 Corinthians 5:7	*"We walk by faith, not by sight."*
Ephesians 2:5	*"You have been saved by God's grace."*

We must always remember that God is in control and is watching over us day and night. We find comfort and peace knowing He is our Father and that He cares us.

THINKING

The Two Moms have been intrigued from the very beginning about this plaque that I have on my wall. It hangs directly in front of me so that I can see it and read it all day long. They really question why it is on a plaque and not just in a frame. Well, I had this plaque with nothing on it just collecting dust and I saved it for something special and important. I don't even remember how long ago I put this together but it is a result of a devotional I read that led me to ask the question, "What are you thinking right now?. I thought that is the perfect thing to put on this plaque and keep in in front of me every day.

Proverbs 23:7 says, *"As a man thinketh in his heart so is he:*

Some of my biggest struggles in my walk with the Lord are a result of my thought life. I am sure there are a few others in this world who can identify with me in this struggle. In fact Scripture talks about our thought life. I believe it is one of the fastest and easiest ways for Satan to attack God's children. The world offers the lust of the eyes, the lust of the flesh and the pride of life. Everything that falls into these three categories are distractions that begin in our thought life. We start looking at, thinking about and dwelling on the things the world has to offer and we soon allow God to be pushed aside in our lives. We have to be careful to control this part of our being or it can and will destroy us. The way we get control of our thought life is found in Romans 12:2 …but let

God transform you into a new person by changing the way you think. This is not a one-time thing, it is a process of daily renewal in our walk with Christ. On that daily journey Paul reminds us in Philippians 4:8 to: think on things that are pure and lovely and admirable, excellent and worthy of praise,

When I find my mind wandering I just look to this plaque on my wall and the question helps me to regain my focus and get my thought life in line with who I am in Christ and what He wants me to be and to do.

TIME

Ephesians 5:16 *"making the best use of the time, because the days are evil."*

If I were to offer you a daily gift of $86,400.00 every morning with one stipulation: you had to use all of it by midnight. You can't save any of it, it must be all gone. Then when the clock strikes midnight, the gift is replenished and you start the process all over again. What would you do with it? You have been given a similar gift that is TIME. Each of us is given this gift in equal proportions: 86,400 seconds in a day. What do you do with that gift? Each second that ticks off the clock is a second won or loss, depending on how you use it. Once it is gone, it can never be redeemed. You cannot save today's seconds for tomorrow. They are all used up at the end of the day. And yet, the gift is replenished and you start all over again. With a new day comes a new gift of TIME. Ask yourself these questions:

- What have you done for someone else today?
- How have you prepared for improvement today?
- How do you want to finish this day with the time you have left?

It is very important that you live in the present. You cannot dwell in the past and live in regret. You cannot peer into the future and live in anxiety. God has given us the present, the time in which you currently live, to live in faith. Make sure you use the time God has given you wisely.

TROPHY

I had the privilege of coaching a group of girl basketball players from around the state of Florida in a Sports Travel adventure for three summers in a row 1996, 1997 and 1998. We traveled oversees to play in some international goodwill type games. We were in Belgium two of those years and Holland for the other. It was a tremendous experience for historical sight- seeing, playing basketball and creating new friendships. We visited Anne Frank's house in Amsterdam, a concentration camp in Belgium, the Eiffel Tower in France, and we played a lot of basketball. Our team took second place in the tournament in both 1997 and 1998. The 1997 was a most memorable tournament as we played in the Friendship Cup in Haarlam, Holland. We compiled a very good team that year and won all the way through the tournament to the championship game. For the championship, we played the Junior National team from Holland and to put it mildly, they were very, very good. Needless to say we took second place to this team and rightfully so. You know it is very tough to put together a team of girls who don't know each other, play in different parts of the state for different coaches with different schemes and do as well as we did. One of the first things we focused upon was team bonding. The second thing we put emphasis upon was each one filling their role and giving 100% for the good of the others. This is especially hard since we had some girls who had signed to play college basketball and were the best players on their teams and in their areas. Everyone had to give up a little bit of themselves in order for the TEAM to be successful.

I Corinthians 9:24-25 – *"Remember that in a race everyone runs, but only one person gets the prize. You must also run in such a way that you will win. All athletes practice strict self-control. They do it to win a prize that will fade away, but we do it for an eternal prize",*

Trophies and accolades have their place in this life, but Paul reminds us that these are only temporal prizes as we run the races and play the games that we do. In running the game of LIFE, we have much more at stake and a greater prize to strive for: an eternal reward. That reward of standing before God and hearing Him say that we have done well. The greatest trophy we could ever give back to God is the one of a life lived serving Him and serving others.

SO, RUN TO WIN!!

UMBRELLA

Yes, I have a collection of umbrellas in my office, because you never know when you will need an umbrella here in Florida. We use an umbrella to protect us from the elements like: rain and sun. Go about your business on a rainy day here in Florida or anywhere for that matter, without an umbrella and see what happens. YOU GET WET! Heck, even with an umbrella here in Florida it seems like you still get wet. Sometimes it seems like the rain is coming down from the sky and coming up from the ground. However, for the most part an umbrella comes in handy and provides protection for us during the rain. The sun is so intense in Florida sometimes, that people will often use an umbrella for protection from the harmful UV rays the sun gives off.

God has made provision for our safety and well-being as He represents an umbrella for our lives. When we stay within the confines of His protective covering, we prosper and do well. It is when we go out from under His covering and provided protection that we find ourselves in trouble. This world will bombard us with continual temptations, trials and testing. We can only stay safe and fight them off when we stay within the guidelines God has provided for us.

Psalm 91

"He that dwelleth in the secret place of the most High shall abide under the shadow of the Almighty.² I will say of the LORD, *He is*

my refuge and my fortress: my God; in him will I trust.³ Surely he shall deliver thee from the snare of the fowler, and from the noisome pestilence.⁴ He shall cover thee with his feathers, and under his wings shalt thou trust: his truth shall be thy shield and buckler.⁵ Thou shalt not be afraid for the terror by night; nor for the arrow that flieth by day;⁶ Nor for the pestilence that walketh in darkness; nor for the destruction that wasteth at noonday.⁷ A thousand shall fall at thy side, and ten thousand at thy right hand; but it shall not come nigh thee.⁸ Only with thine eyes shalt thou behold and see the reward of the wicked.⁹ Because thou hast made the LORD, which is my refuge, even the most High, thy habitation;¹⁰ There shall no evil befall thee, neither shall any plague come nigh thy dwelling.¹¹ For he shall give his angels charge over thee, to keep thee in all thy ways.¹² They shall bear thee up in their hands, lest thou dash thy foot against a stone.¹³ Thou shalt tread upon the lion and adder: the young lion and the dragon shalt thou trample under feet.¹⁴ Because he hath set his love upon me, therefore will I deliver him: I will set him on high, because he hath known my name.¹⁵ He shall call upon me, and I will answer him: I will be with him in trouble; I will deliver him, and honour him.¹⁶ With long life will I satisfy him, and shew him my salvation.

For your ultimate protection, stay under His covering and live life to the fullest.

VALUES

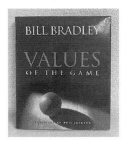

I probably have over 200 books in my library here in my office and on the bookshelf at home. Books ranging in subjects from self-help to biographies to strategies to books with funny titles. Of all the books I have read and that are on my shelves, this one is a favorite of mine. Bill Bradley played professional basketball and was a pretty good player. He was a leader on his team and played the game with heart and hustle. He outlines several values that he has observed and or has put into practice in his life. I personally have written and published two books of my own, "Before the Whistle: Motivation and Inspiration to get you started" and "Five Smooth Stones: Proven Steps for Positive Success". In my book "Five Smooth Stones" I outline five important steps, stones or values to running a team, a corporation or for success in everyday living.

1. Bring your "A" game every day. In other words, do your best, give 100% in everything you do every day.

2. Little things make a difference – make sure to take care of the little things on a consistent basis.

3. Treat others the way you want to be treated – putting others first and treating them with respect

4. Leave a place better than the way you found it – have class, make things better.

5. Influence others – leave a lasting impression to impact others in a positive way.

These are the core values I have as a coach for every team I have ever coached. They are great values to have no matter what you do, where you go or who you are.

Romans 12 is my favorite chapter in the Bible. Paul gives us several values to live by in this chapter:

Use our abilities, love genuinely, work hard, be patient, help others, don't act important, don't think you know it all, live in peace with everyone.

WHAT ARE THE CORE VALUES THAT YOU HAVE ADOPTED FOR LIVING YOUR LIFE TO THE FULLEST?

VISION

A strange phenomenom takes place from birth to middle-age: our eyesight deteriorates and we need help with our vision. I currently use 1.5 strength readers so I can see written words up close. I don't have trouble reading signs and things from afar, but to read a book or my Bible, I need help. Vision is one of the more important of our senses. We can certainly live without it, but it sure makes life easier having it in good working order. Good vision has an effect on and in everything we do.

Physical Vision – being able to actually see with our own eyes. The colors, shapes and sizes of things we encounter in everyday life. We use visual aids to help us see clearly with sharp focus.

Virtual Vision – being able to see in the mind's eye or project in your mind what you can and should do in a given scenario. Being able to make discernment and judgements base on what conclusions you come to in your mind as you envision the scenario. For instance I tell my players to shoot virtual free throws. You don't need a ball or a basket. But you go through your routine with your eyes closed shoot your free throws with proper technique and see the ball going into the basket.

Practical Vision – setting goals and the course of action for success in business, sports, and life. Being able to see a final result and then plotting a course to achieve that result. As coaches we game plan, strategize and set goals for the season, each game and every practice. Then we set out to accomplish the goals with a plan and a purpose

These are by no means scientific definitions, they are what I perceive in my head. You can call them what you want and you can add any other type of vision that you can think of. However, the point is that you need clarity and focus in your vision whether it be in a physical sense or a practical sense.

> Proverbs 29:18 *"Where there is no **vision**, the people perish: but he that keepeth the law, happy is he."*

YARDSTICK

The yardstick is a device used in measuring things. Units of measure have been around since the beginning of time. Noah use some type of measuring device in building the ark. The ancient Babylonians improved the methods of measure they evolved over time. In the early 1300's King Edward decided there should be some universal measure and adopted what we now know as the yard stick. It was originally called the "iron ulna" basically after the ulna bone in the arm. He also decreed that the foot measure be one third of a yard. Thus we got a more standard unit of measure.

I have read about "the measure of a man". I have heard speakers refer to the "measure of a man". The world offers up different standards of measurements for living life. The Bible clearly states that what the world offers will only end in destruction. We also find that God has standards of measurement for each of His children.

> Romans 12:3 *"....be honest in your estimate of yourselves measuring your value by how much faith God has given you."*

Paul was dealing with a plethora of issues from carnal Christianity to the Pharisees who put undue pressures on the Christians of that day. Especially the unnecessary requirements they used to measure spirituality in everyone.

II Corinthians 10:12-13 *"….these other men who tell you how important they are! But they are only comparing themselves with each other and measuring themselves by themselves. What foolishness!"*

But we will not boast of authority we do not have. Our goal is to stay within the boundaries of God's plan for us.

God's measure is so completely different than the world's. He measures us thru His son Jesus. He measures us by how much faith we have in Him. He measure us by what we do with the gifts, talents and abilities that He has given us.

Let us stay within the boundaries of God's love and provision so that when we are measured, we measure up to His standards.

The person who removes a mountain begins
by carrying away small stones

CONCLUSION

The gauntlet was thrown down and the challenge was met. There are object lessons in random objects if you look hard enough for them. Sometimes it comes really easily and other times you have to get creative to make the correlation to a spiritual application. God designed, created and built this world and all that is in it. Every single thing has His fingerprints all over it. From the universe, the ground, the sky, the vegetation, the animals and the humans. All was designed with purpose and significance. The goal of this book is to help you to see His handiwork in the simplest of things and to realize how great a Father we have in Heaven. He tells us how much He loves us and has shown us in thousands of ways how deep that love runs. In return we are to love God and love others. Open your eyes and look around and intentionally look for Him in everything you see.

What lies behind us and what lies before us are
small matters to what lies within us.

ABOUT THE AUTHOR

Phil Farver is the oldest of four children from a preacher's family in Michigan. He attended Maranatha Baptist Bible College in Wisconsin and graduated with a degree in Bible and PE. He has been married to his wife Rhonda for 43 years. They have two children, Kindal and Blake. They now have three grandchildren, Ivy, Layla and Asher. Phil has been a teacher, coach and Athletic Director for 44 years and has a wide array of talent and ability. He has authored two books, *"Five Smooth Stones: Proven steps for positive success",* and *"Before the Whistle: Inspiration and motivation to get you started".* His work ethic is consistent and he is unwavering in who he is and what he has been called to do. His strongest desire is to be a positive influence on everyone he coaches and works with.